Murphy and His Friends Learn to Count From 1 to 10

Written by: Cynthia Scott Griffin   Illustrated by: Megan Dodge Sergi

Murphy and His Friends Learn to Count From 1 to 10
All Rights Reserved.
Copyright © 2015 Cynthia Scott Griffin and Megan Dodge Sergi
v1.0

Griffin Publishing

ISBN: 978-0-578-16400-7

Library of Congress Control Number: 2015907548

PRINTED IN THE UNITED STATES OF AMERICA

Oscar the ornery octopus with one orb

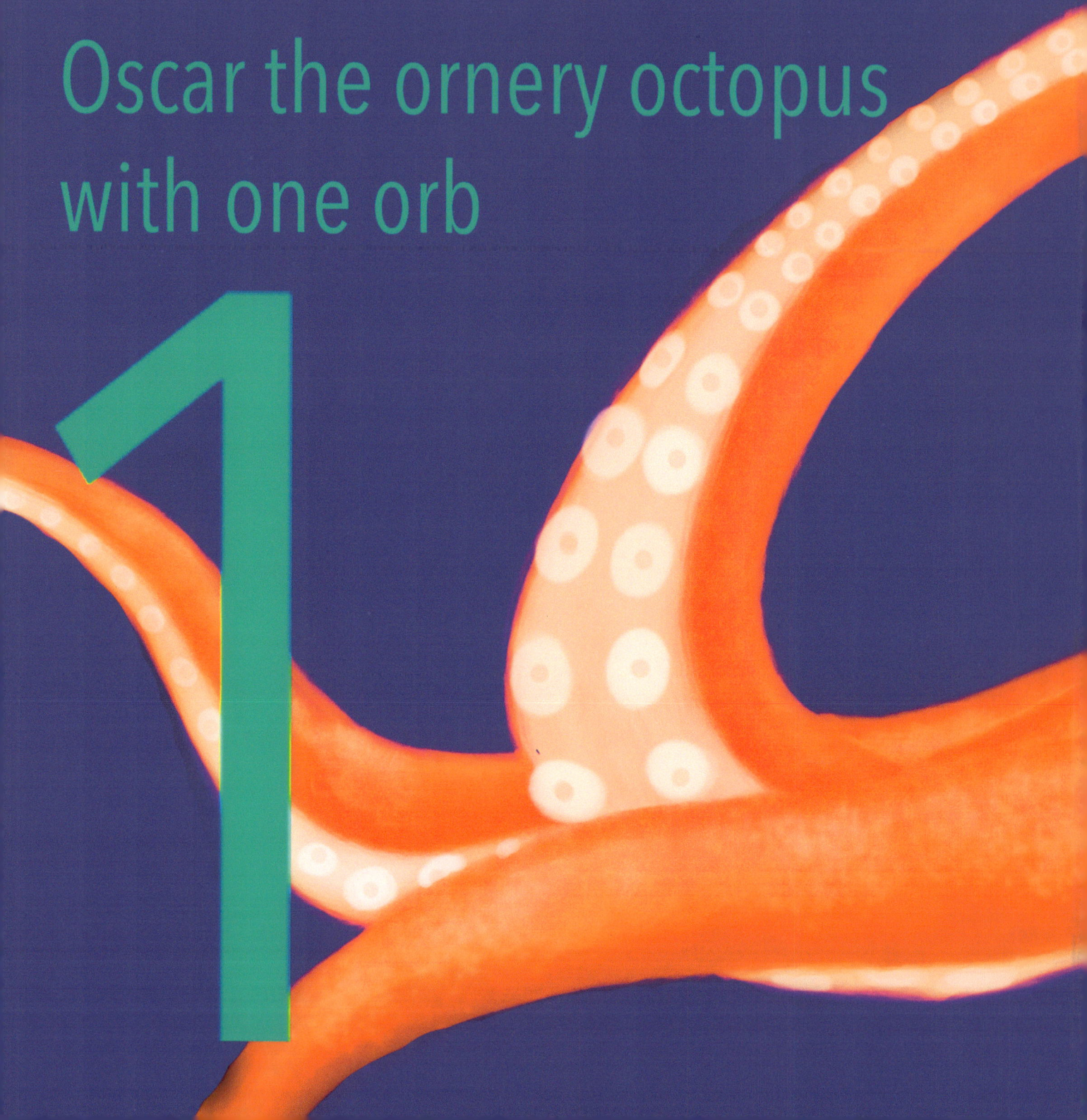

1

Murphy the magnificent moose with two magnifying glasses

2

Julie the jaunty jackrabbit
with three jagged jewels

3

Frederick the fairytale frog with four fine fish

4

Quinnie the Queen quail quietly cuddling her five quintuplets

5

Sandy the sneaky snake hiding six silver spoons

6

Charlie the chunky chipmunk eating seven chocolate chip cookies

7

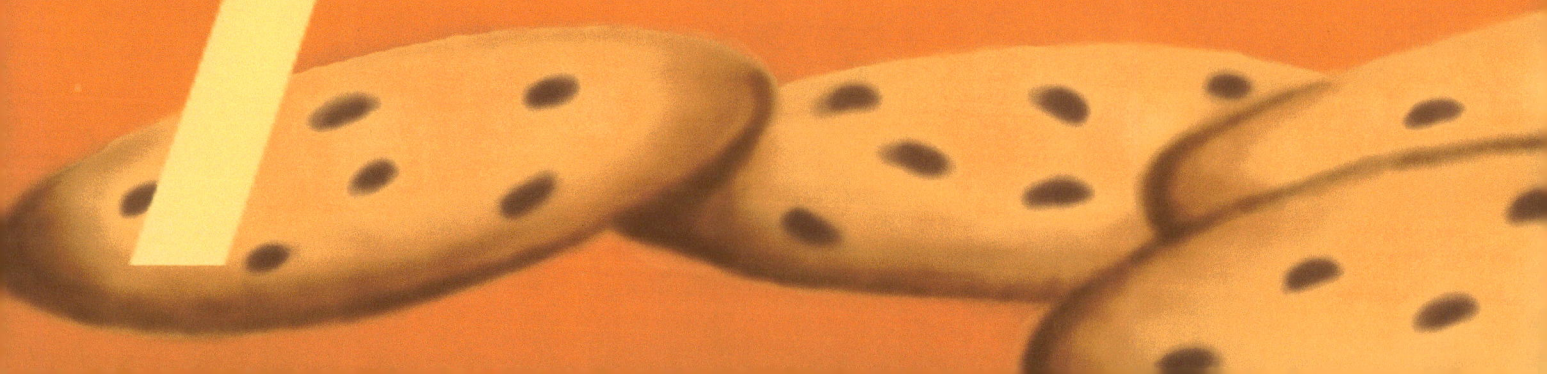

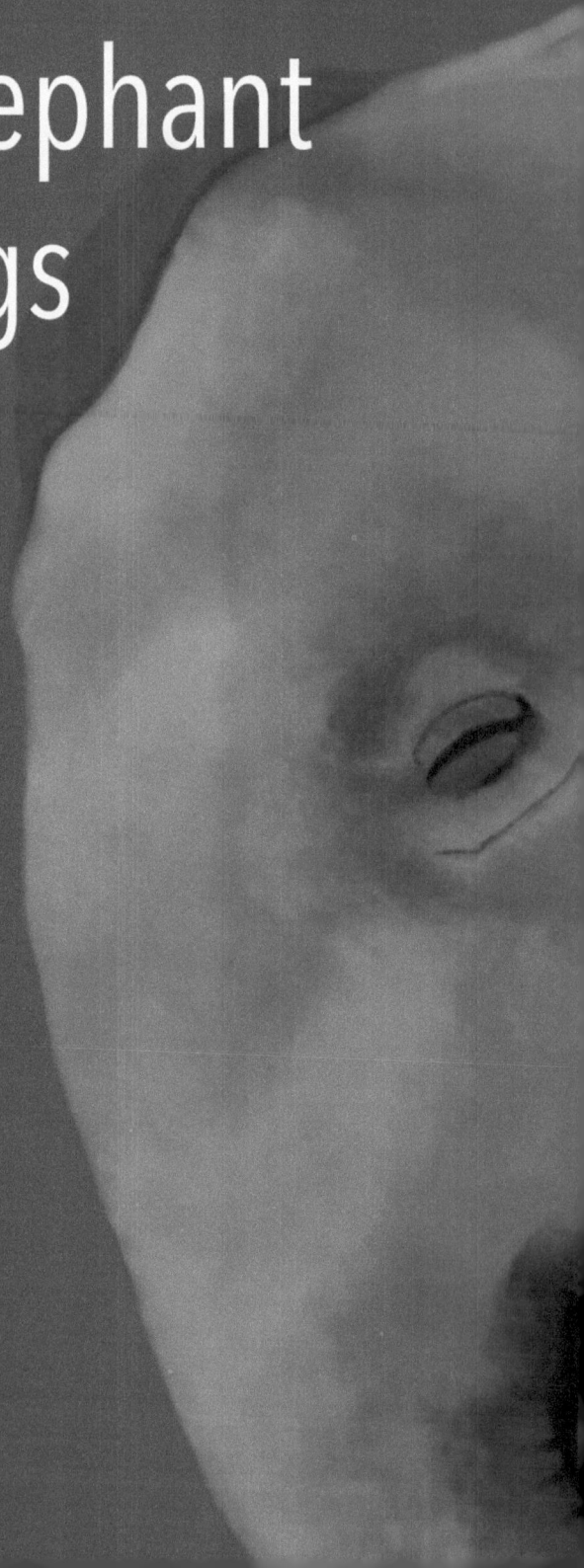

Ella the elegant elephant cuddling eight eggs

8

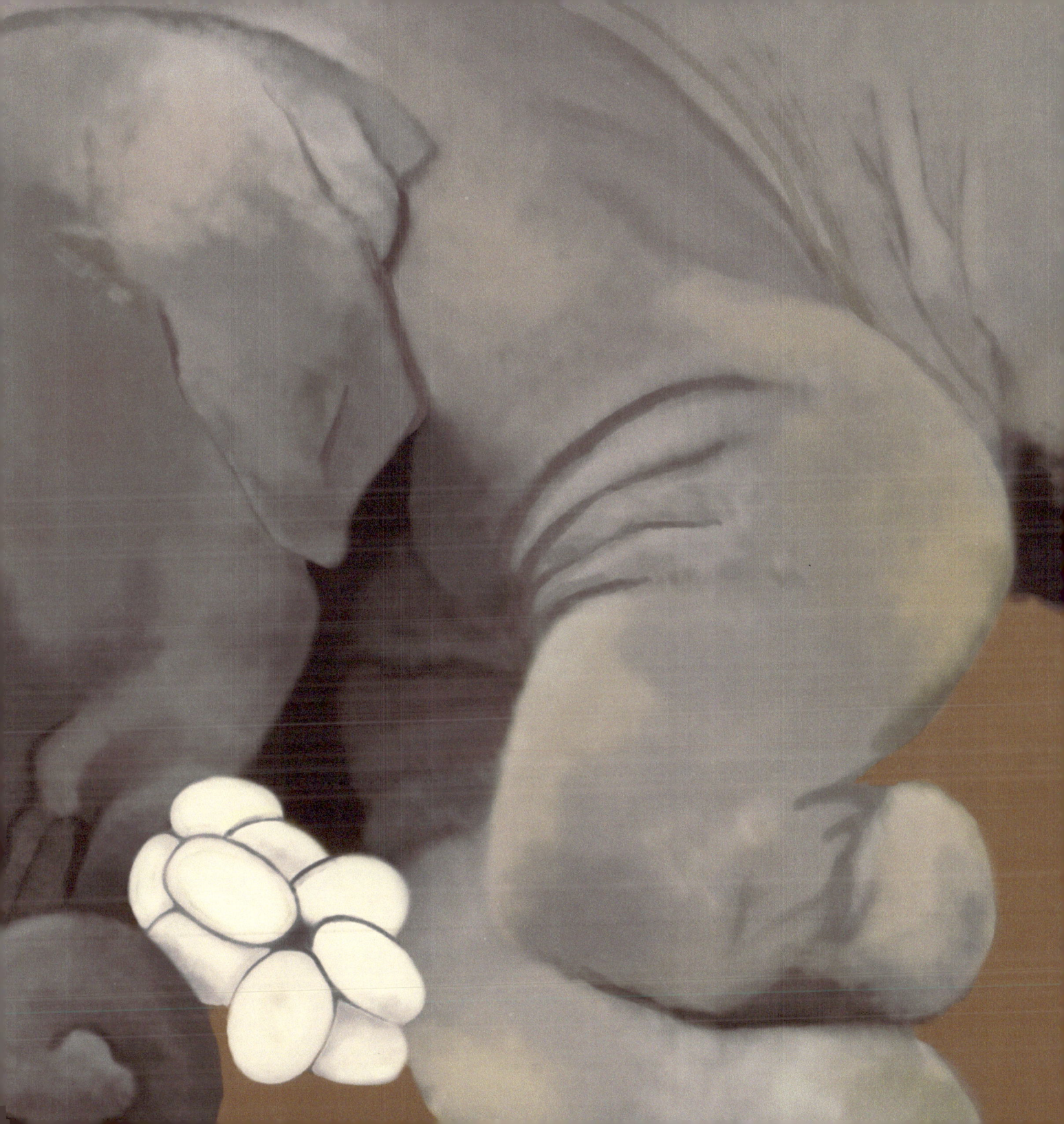

Norman the naughty newt with nine nickels

9

Trevor the tired tiger
with ten teacups

10

www.ingramcontent.com/pod-product-compliance
Lightning Source LLC
LaVergne TN
LVHW072123070426
835511LV00002B/79